Live,
Laugh,
Love,
While You Can!

My Journey Through Stuttering, Love, Church & School

Matthew Bacchus

Compiled and Edited
by
Franzeska Sampson, MSW, EdD (C)
Published by TCOOMH INC.
Tcoomh2019@gmail.com,   Fransamp.org

Cover design
by
Quenice B. Coaxum
Qdesigns Media Co.
www.QCoaxum.com

Live, Love, Laugh! While you can.

Dedication

I dedicate this book to all who experience hurt, pain, trauma and still deal with it. I dedicate this book to those who stutter. I want you to know that you can be anything you want to be. You can achieve great things. To those who have a story to tell and are afraid to share, know that sharing your story can bring you deliverance, heal others and give God glory. This book is for you.

Live,
Laugh,
Love,
While You Can!

Contents

Acknowledgments

I would like to acknowledge first and foremost my Lord and Savior, Jesus Christ, without him, I am nothing, and this book wouldn't be possible. He helped me through the different experiences I have encountered. I thank him for everything. Secondly, I would like to thank my parents. I'm blessed to have them with me. I am the man I've become because of their example and what they have modeled before me. There is no Matthew Bacchus without Michael and Patricia Bacchus. I thank God for them, and I honor them. Lastly, I thank God for my friends and family. Too many to name, and I don't want to get in trouble. You know who you are and how much you mean to me. I thank you for sticking with me, loving me, and helping me in your unique way. Many times, you have helped me through my difficulties, and I will forever be thankful.

Foreword

My family and I attended the Brooklyn Campus of Full Gospel Assembly for several years. I was familiar with all of our senior Pastor Michael Bacchus and Sister Patricia Bacchus's children. At least that's what I thought. Reflecting, I did not recall ever having an encounter with Matthew. If I did it was probably so brief that I did not recall. One afternoon; I was sitting at the back of the church alone, waiting for my son, who was rehearsing for fine arts. A young man approached me to inquire whether I was a parent waiting on one of the youths. I responded yes, and we started a conversation. One of my comments to Matthew was, I don't recall seeing you before? He chuckled and gave that smile like he usually does. That was the beginning of a beautiful friendship. Matthew and I have spent numerous hours talking about everything under the sun. Life, experiences, disappointments, hurts, pains, personal plans, career goals, and aspirations, you name it, we have spoken about it.

As I began to know Matthew, one of the things I realized almost immediately was that his aspirations and goals were remarkable and significant. He had the ideas but was afraid to step out on them. Something was holding him back. One particular goal we discussed was establishing a non-profit organization. I was immediately obliged to assist. In 2019, Matthew started his non-profit organization, Helping Others Meet Expectations (HOME). To date,

HOME has provided scholarships to high school graduates entering college, donated supplies to public schools and homeless shelters in New York City and collaborated with other organizations to benefit the community and underserved populations. Our friendship grew tremendously over the years. Matthew is one of the kindest, most genuine, and loving people anyone would encounter. He has had plans, visions, dreams, goals, and aspirations for years and, as discussed in this book, did not step out to accomplish them due to fear of a speech impediment. There were times when I pressed him a bit hard to step up and step out on his remarkable ideas. He sometimes got annoyed, and I let the issue slide for a while before revisiting the topic.

Matthew has a story to tell. The world is waiting for these ideas, which he has given birth to. This book is just the beginning. I am thrilled that he has decided to share his story with the world because there is deliverance for others in our pain. As you read this book, identify areas where you hurt, felt, or are feeling crippled and are afraid to venture out. This book is for you. The goal of this book is to dialogue about those things that hurt, cripple, and keep us stagnant. Everyone has an area of struggle. Identify your pain, use tools and resource available to you to work through your pain, and then use your story as a testimony to help others.

Franzeska

Introduction

Live, Laugh, Love, While You Can: My journey through Stuttering, Love, Church, and School, is an intimate and transparent look at my life. In this book, I share my hurt, pain, anguish, and traumatic experiences over the years while on the journey to finding myself. This book gives you an intimate look at who Matthew Bacchus is. I am a friend, lover, a sensual and tantalizing writer. Live, Laugh, Love, While You Can, provides a map for anyone who has experienced self-doubt at any given point in their lives and thought they were not worthy or even questioned existing in this world. In this book, I go in-depth about the hurt and pain I experience because of a speech impediment. In my first book, "My Poetry, My Story, My Testimony, For His Glory," I shared through poetry what I faced growing up. I can honestly say God got me through it all. God can get you through whatever hinders you from moving forward. Take the necessary steps to get back to your happy place. Make moves that excite you. Go places that bring joy to your life. Go see a movie. I thank God for the people I have surrounding me. This book is here to bring healing to many.

God's Plan Hurts

Surrendering your agenda to pick up his

Going through twists

Going through turns

Many lessons learned

You flee from Nineveh

Thinking you will get away

Not knowing there's a price to be paid

God's plan hurts

Shake you and break you

Remake you

Clay, you're in the potter's hands

Interrupting your plans

You don't stand a chance

Doors begin to close

Trying to reach your goals

Feeling God is moving slow

But God is in control

He will tell you to go

Ask Abraham about leaving his familiar

To a land, God will show

Having to trust him in the unknown

Bow your will

Your flesh he will kill

Chisel some things off you

God's plan hurts

Making your life brand new

Your plans are screwed

Your life he uses

Take you through your own Gethsemane

But in the end, there's the victory

God's plan hurts

Your life is not your own

God is first

God will do whatever it takes, even if it hurts

Living Or Existing

There were times in my life when I did not want to live or exist. Those who stutter or have a disability can understand or relate to this perspective. Growing up with a speech impediment and the inability to communicate the way I wanted was a significant problem for me. I would often ponder questions such as, why live? Or why face this issue in my life? The only way to be free and not hurt was to end it. I had suicidal thoughts and ideations. I did not want to suffer through life like this anymore. This is not fair! Why me? That is what I used to ask myself. I dealt with bullying at school and often did not fit in to socialize with my peers. For many years I had low self-esteem. I didn't believe in myself. I kept to myself and did not speak much. I was afraid of being exposed and hurt repeatedly. I carried so much hurt and pain with me into my adult life and allowed myself to be imprisoned. I didn't have the strength or courage to move beyond my experiences. I was bound to my past while simultaneously having the desire to be free. The only way for me to be free was to let go. Let go of past pain, hurt, disappointments, and not living up to my or others' expectations. Letting go of my past wasn't very easy for me. I allowed thoughts and memories of my past to haunt me and interfere with my forward progress. I could be so far ahead in life if I had only made up my mind to be free. Often in life, we are bounded by our experience.

Experiences that God has forgiven us from, people have moved on, and we yet remain bounded, stagnant, and unmotivated. Are you free today? Free from the opinions of people? Are you free from the hurt and pain you experienced yesterday? Have you allowed it to interfere with your today? I had to realize that time is precious. I can continue to feel sorry for myself, stay where I currently am, or decide to pick myself up and go in the direction of living. I have so much to live for. So much I want to accomplish. I cannot allow a speech impediment to hinder my growth and where I want to go. I have visions and goals. I must be strong mentally. Strong and brave to look past the ridicule, things that occurred, and what is ahead. I realized that while feeling sorry for myself or down on myself, people were still living their lives.

People often don't care about how you feel and what you are experiencing. They are doing what is best for them. I have realized that I must do what is best for me. I have an I don't care about my past attitude now. **I will go scared. I will go afraid. I will just go.** I must live my best life and do what is necessary to win. I don't want to live a defeated life. You shouldn't either. Someone is waiting for what you have to offer. You can change a life today despite where you are. I realized that the longer I take to understand who I am and what I can accomplish, the longer someone doesn't receive what they need.

We are the answer to many problems in the world. Despite any form of disability, you can make a difference. I can make a difference. You just need to decide. The choice is yours. I had to choose to live a defeated or a victorious life. Tomorrow is not guaranteed to us. One minute we are here, and the next minute we are not. The wealthiest place in the world is the cemetery. So many gifted people died with their gifts tucked away inside of them. We are living for a cause much greater than ourselves. We are here to present something marvelous to the table and the world that will make a difference, impact, and change lives. **Find your gift. Find your calling. Find what you were born to do.** Throughout my struggle, I have found what I love to do. Writing is my passion and the thing that helped me get through the hard times. I found writing was my escape from the hurt and pain caused by others. Sometimes you birth your gifts through difficult times. Writing poetry gives me comfort. I felt like I was finally living when I began writing. Writing was my escape from the world. While writing, I had no one judging me, no one looking at me funny, and I could say whatever I wanted without talking. I grew up in church. My dad is the Senior Pastor of Full Gospel Assembly. Many times, at church, I would ask my dad to read my poems during service. I was too afraid to speak in front of the congregation because I felt that I would be judged.

I later realized that although poetry was my escape, I hid behind my writing. I use writing as my crutch. Writing poetry was my way of being free, but I was allowing it to hinder my forward progress.

Reflecting now with a different attitude and perspective on life, I can go forward, live my life, and be happy. Writing this book and sharing my story makes me happy, knowing that my mission will be accomplished if I touch one life and change one life for the better. Your purpose in life may very well be associated with the pain you've experienced. I realize that I can use my pain for good. How can your pain be used for good? I want you to think about that for a moment. What can you create out of your bad experiences? Can your hurt and pain generate wealth for you? What are you doing with your pain? You can't carry around that hurt and pain. Pain is toxic to your life. To live, you got to be free from toxic things. Unforgiveness is a toxic thing that can stop you from living the life you want. Unforgiveness is like drinking poison and expecting the other person to die.

Are you living or existing? My definition of living is doing what your heart desire, fulfilling all you want to do, and not allowing anything or anyone to hold you back. Existing is not fulfilling your God-given purpose, accepting life the way it is, and not being willing to do what is necessary to enjoy life. For most of my life, I felt like I was just existing and not living. I was so focused on the speech impediment that I failed to appreciate life. I fail to focus on the positive things. I didn't think my life mattered. I felt sorry for myself. I began to ask myself, what was wrong with me? Why was I put here to suffer like this? At one point, I didn't want to be here because I wanted to be what I deemed "normal." I wanted to be just like everyone else. I tried to talk without people looking at me strangely or weirdly. I did not want to answer questions such as: Why do you speak this way? What is wrong with you? For many years I had a victim mentality. I didn't see myself as worthy of living. I've experienced depression at various times during my life. I wanted to change but felt that change was never going to come. I had breath in my body, but I wasn't living. I was just existing. I didn't see myself making a difference in the world. That was my problem. I didn't see beyond my disability. I didn't see myself as someone who could become great. I didn't realize that I was wasting precious time focusing on my issue. I had to change my thinking. I had to ask myself what I wanted to do with my life. I will ask you the same question. **What do you want to do with your life?**

Have you settled because your disability has crippled you mentally? There is power in your thoughts, your mind. Have you counted yourself out because you feel you're not worthy enough or good enough to become great at what you want to do? We can be our own worst enemy just by the way we think. We can talk ourselves out of being great. We often focus and worry about the opinions of others. We conclude things in our minds that cause us to not push forward with what we desire. At various times, I failed to step out on faith to do what I wanted because I kept living in the past. I kept remembering all the hurt and pain I experienced growing up. People pointing, laughing, making fun of my speech, and I allow their thoughts and opinions to control my thinking and my life. Have you allowed someone's thoughts or opinions of you to control your life? Are you comfortable where you are, or is there something you want to do and you're afraid? My dream is to write. I put it off for a long time because I was too scared or afraid to speak. I felt writing would lead to talking. I didn't want to let go of my past hurt and pain and focus on the future. **I nurtured and nourished the past.** You must let go of your past to embrace your future. What happened yesterday cannot be changed. You can only focus on today so that you can live and enjoy life. I felt I wasn't important or significant, so I stayed where I was. Don't stay where you are. There is a purpose and a plan for your life. Find your passion. Find what you are good at and work at it. Don't settle where you are.

Are you living or existing? What is your dream? If money wasn't an issue, what would you want to be? What is the thing that keeps you up at night? I say to you that today you are living for a cause much greater than yourself. You weren't put here on earth by chance. There is something great for you to do. Find that out and work at it. Failing to plan is to plan to fail. Proverbs 21:5 (NJKV) tells us that the plans of the diligent lead surely to plenty, but those of everyone who is hasty surely to poverty. You must have a plan. That is your first step. Your next step is to write it out. Make your vision plain. Habakkuk 2:2,3 (NJKV). The next part is to pray and act on your plan. Faith without works is dead. James 2:14 (NJKV). Don't be afraid to ask for help. I have goals and dreams I want to accomplish, but I was too scared to act. I was so focused on my speech that everything else in my life became secondary. I allowed my speech impediment to cripple me. I had to realize that to accomplish my dream, I must step out of my comfort zone. We will talk about comfort zone in one of the later chapters.

Part of living entails doing what you love and enjoying life. You only have one shot at this life; **Make it grand.** What gets you going in the morning? What is that one thing that you look forward to doing each day? Just think for a moment. We are all on a time clock. There is a time that we will no longer be here. The only two things guaranteed in life are "death and taxes." Make a change today. Commit to writing your vision and making it plain. I suggest getting accountability partners. Real partners who won't be afraid to tell you to get up from where you are and move into what you are supposed to. Don't surround yourself with yes people. Surround yourself with partners who will help you get to where you are trying to go. Do you know that people are waiting to receive the gift you have in your head? That thing you've been thinking about can help others. There are people waiting for you to live so you can produce what has been burning on the inside of you. Will you make a change today? Change from existing to living.

Key Points

Don't allow your disability to cripple you mentally.

Moving from existing to living requires actions.

There are people waiting for you to live.

Suggestions for Living

Do things that make you want to live.

Renew your mind daily with positive thoughts.

List the things you want to accomplish and act.

Prayer

Father God, I pray for those who are dying on the inside. I pray for those who have no desire to live. I pray for those who don't know their purpose. I pray you give them a vision today. I pray you visit them. I pray you meet them wherever they will be reading this. I pray your angel encamps around them. I pray you will rejuvenate them. Show them your perfect plan for their lives. I pray against those who spoke negatively about their lives. I speak life to every part of you. You will live and not die. You will be the head and not the tail. Your life is important. You are special in the sight of God. You will do great exploit. I pray for those who keep falling. I pray for those who keep making wrong choices. I pray for those who just can't seem to get it right. Holy Spirit reminds them that they exist for a greater purpose. May they learn what that is today and walk in it. In Jesus' Name Amen.

<u>Living Versus Existing</u>

Trying to live and not just exist

Changing my mindset

I want to live

Letting go of the pain of yesterday

I want to be free

Free from yesterday

Today, I am free

I choose to be happy

Choosing to be me

Wanting to bring healing to many

Wanting to bring change

Even if that means talking about my pain

Talking about me

Talking about the things that hurt me

I allow the spirit of fear to take control

It held me back from accomplishing my goals

Not anymore

I had enough of this

I don't just want to exist

I want to live!

<u>Why Am I Here?</u>

Why am I here?

I cried so many tears

I had some difficult years

What was I brought here to do?

Why this pain?

Where is the sunshine?

Why all this rain?

What is my purpose?

What is the purpose of this hurt?

I don't want to waste my time

I want to be exactly where I need to be

God, please take the lead

My life is not going my way

My plans are falling apart

Then I hear you say

My thoughts are not your thoughts

My ways are not your ways

All these cloudy days

Wanting this to go away

Wanting this never to return

What lesson must I learn?

Why am I here?

Am I near?

Near my destination

Is there more to experience?

God, are you listening?

Will my pain make a difference?

I need to hear

Why am I here?

<u>**My Peace Is Everything**</u>

My peace is everything

I've experienced a lot on this journey

I realize what's good for me

Being free mentally is key

I no longer aim to please

I'm focused on being healthy

Emotionally, Spiritually, Physically, and Mentally

most of my life was well spent

Doing for others

I put on the shelf my wellness

I had some regrets

I live and learn

Now I discern

Discern what or who enters my place

Protecting my space

My peace is everything

I learned that I could do without so many things

I choose peace, love, happiness, joy and wellness.

My Silent Scream

I've experienced a lot living with a speech impediment. I didn't wear my hurt and pain. Like many, I kept everything on the inside. No one could hear my silent scream. I pretended that everything was ok, and I did my best not to think about this issue, but the only place I could scream was on the inside. No one could hear my heart cry. Can you hear the silent scream of the one you love? Can you hear the ones who cry themselves to sleep because of the issue or issues they are going through every day? I'm thankful for the friends that called or texted me to see how I am doing. Many times, I wasn't ok, and to hear their voice or to hang out was what got me through so many times, and they didn't even know it. I live most of my life being strong. Strong enough to carry the burdens or issues of those who confided in and shared personal things with me. I had to train my mind to stay positive despite feeling like I was dying on the inside. You will be amazed by the number of people who walk around dressing nice, smiles on their faces; everything seems to be going fine, but, on the inside, they are screaming for help. Many felt that people would not get it. People don't understand. I've felt that way sometimes. People just don't get how hard it is to deal with challenges. I'm sure that others can testify of this issue and say the same thing. Pay attention to the things people are not saying. You must be in tune with those you are around. Everyone is not ok. Most people are fighting a battle that you don't see. Take time to spend time with those you are connected to and to make sure they are doing fine. Before there was a suicide, there was a silent scream. You find many stories of people who committed suicide and how they appeared fine to people. They didn't show any sign of anything being wrong. So many are dealing with thoughts that are unhealthy. Never become too busy for friends and loved ones. You might be saving a life.

Key Points

Everyone may look ok, but many are holding on by a thread.

Stress, fear, and anxiety can be a killer.

A silent scream can leave you hopeless and helpless.

Suggestions for Staying Connected

Be a person that someone can talk to without judgment.

Make an effort to listen to the things that are not expressed verbally

Check-in on your friends and family often.

Prayer

Father, I pray for those who are suffering silently. I pray for those hurting on the inside, and no one knows about it. I pray you meet them where they are today. You are our all in all. You know all things. You know the real us. Heal and set them free today. Restore them. I pray for restoration today. I pray for Joy. May your joy be their strength today. Help them through the healing process. Gentle Shepherd lead today and remind them that they don't have to suffer in silent anymore. In Jesus' Name Amen.

Silent Scream

Walking around like everything is ok

Just look at the suicide rates

Many are dying every day

No one can hear their silent scream

Happy they seem

You wouldn't believe

The pain they feel

Many are hurting

They just want to be healed

Fighting through negative thoughts

Counting the cost

The price of their pain

While wanting change

Wanting the pain to go away

Gun to the brain

Silent scream

Walking this lonely road

While still wanting to accomplish some goals

The issue hurt the soul

Silent scream

Invisible bruises and scars

You can't even see them bleed

If you're really paying attention

You can hear their silent scream

My Mental Health

Trauma is a deeply distressing or disturbing experience. Two places I felt that my trauma was ongoing were school and church. There was a continuous need and requirement for me to speak. To do well in school, I had to participate. Some classes have requirements of doing presentations or speaking in front of the class at different times. I was often called upon to participate in various programs and activities at church. Being the son of a Pastor intensified my engagement requirements. I recalled a time at school when my class had to put our desks in a circle, and each student had to read a passage from the assigned book. I immediately decided that I needed to go to the bathroom. I recall another time when I ordered my food in a fast-food restaurant. I told the young lady I wanted a Sprite. She kept asking me to repeat myself, saying she did not understand me. I kept repeating myself, and she kept asking. Finally, another person told her what I was saying. I felt embarrassed and hurt, all at the same time. In church, it was a little different. I would be asked to do something on a special program, such as say a prayer or a poem. At that moment, I would say sure I would do it; but leading up to the appointed time, I made sure I was nowhere in sight or made up an excuse. In my mind, I didn't want to do any talking at all. I just wanted to be left alone. A part of me felt bad because I like doing things. However, I felt like I was being held back by continuously being put in the spotlight. I love serving God and helping wherever I can. However, I did not want to face anything involving talking because of fear of embarrassment. I'm thankful for my experiences and memories because they will help others get through. Whatever trauma you face in life, and you can't shake it or try to forget it, **give it to God, and let Him use your story for his glory.**

Your laugh matters. Laughter is good medicine for your soul. Growing up, I had to laugh my hurt and pain away. When I was constantly being made fun of, I had to laugh, so that I didn't cry or hurt someone. It was very hurtful when I was made fun of. For a long time, I had to hide those feelings. So many don't know what it was like to walk in my shoes. You may tell yourself, I can identify with your hurt and pain, and I've been there. Throughout my life, I had to learn to keep things inside. The fear of expressing how I felt held me back. I had to learn to surround myself with people who genuinely didn't care how I spoke. I had to surround myself with people who made me laugh. People who accepted me for who I am. Your laugh matters. I had to learn to take my mind off my issue and focus on enjoying life. I had to learn to laugh. Learn to breathe.

I had to allow the Joy of the lord to be my strength. I ask you today. What has taken your Joy that you no longer laugh? What has taken away your smile? For a long time, I was smiling on the outside, but on the inside, I was struggling. I wanted the thought of stuttering to exit my life forever. I had to learn to accept that it was not going anywhere. I had to live with it. I had a choice to either let it rob me of my joy or just live life and laugh. I had to learn to do things and be around people who make me laugh. It helps me to take my mind off things. Help me to enjoy the beauty of life. I was so focused and obsessed with the issue that I missed out on precious moments, precious things that matter.

You may say I don't have any reason to laugh. My life is terrible. My life is worthless. There is nothing to live for, might be your thoughts. You have so much to live for. Your flaw and your issues are not the ends of the world. Yes, there is some adjusting. Yes, there are some things you got to deal with that others don't, but "You" determine how your life will turn out. It's all about your mindset. Your choices you make. I could choose to dwell on a speech impediment, or I can live the best life. Think about all the things you hope or wish to do in your lifetime and make them happen. It becomes easier to take one step at a time and not rush the process. Enjoy the journey and turn your pain into power. I had to also learn that people aren't going to feel sorry for me. I had to stop allowing my speech impediment to be a crutch. I had to stop making excuses. Even writing this book was hard for me. In this book, I go in-depth about the hurt and pain I experience because of stuttering. In my first book, "My Poetry, My Story, My Testimony, For His Glory," I shared through poetry what I faced growing up. I can honestly say God got me through it all. God can get you through whatever hinders you from moving forward.

Take the necessary steps to get back to your happy place. Make moves that excite you. Go places that bring joy to your life. Go see a movie. Go to a comedy show. Go to places that bring peace to your life and mind. I thank God for the people I have around me. They helped me take my mind off things. The late Arthur Fletcher from the United Negro College Fund stated that the mind is a terrible thing to waste. I wasted so much time thinking I wasn't good enough. I wasn't worthy to receive love and be accepted. It's important that you train your mind for the positive. You must look within yourself and see what makes you happy. What makes you smile? What makes you wake up each morning? You got to work at being better emotionally and mentally. **I must do that each day! You can't allow what you're facing to win! No more losing! It's winning season! Take your joy back! Take your peace back! Take your laughter back!**

Begin to think of something or some things that make you smile or laugh. Dwell on it if you must. You heal yourself when you laugh. Laughter causes you to forget your problem or issue, even if it is just for a moment. Put yourself in an environment that creates joy, peace, happiness, and laughter. Positive energy is necessary for where you're going. Don't surround yourself with people who are always negative, nothing positive, always serious, and never smile. Beware of those people.

Key Points

Some painful memories will never go away.

Some traumas can affect your forward progress.

What people say and do can cause damage to your mental health.

Do things that will bring laughter to your life.

Protect your mind and space always.

Laughter brings healing to your life.

Suggestions for Working Through Your Pain

Share your story with others; you never know who you're helping.

Be there for someone hurting, and you will find your healing.

Do something great for those who've experienced trauma.

Attend a comedy show.

Watch something that is funny.

Connect with someone funny and great to be around.

Prayer

Father, I pray for the mental well-being of all. Touch those fighting through negative thoughts. Touch those dealing with painful memories of their past hurt and experiences. I pray you heal and give them peace of mind. Renew their mind with positive things. I pray you help them to let go and let you have your way. I pray you touch their thought life. I pray you refresh them today. I pray you help them to move forward to greater things. I pray for those who feel stuck. I pray for those who feel less than. I pray for those who don't feel worthy. I pray for those trying to do the best they can to be better. Have your way today father. In Jesus' Name Amen.

Healing Of My Mind

Healing of my mind

I walked around with a smile

Pretending like everything is fine

Remembering the nights I cried

I was wondering why

Why Is this my life?

Trying to navigate

Wondering if it was too late

To make changes to my thinking

Having to change my stinking thinking

I felt like I was sinking

Wondering if God was hearing

Hearing my silent scream

Like Martin Luther King Jr

I have a dream

I allowed my negative thinking to take hold of me

One day a light dawned on me

I didn't care anymore

I am free

The opinions of people no longer bother me

I walk in freedom

I walk in victory

Healing of my mind

Healing is mine

<u>No Laughing Matter</u>

Feeling my speech was a disaster

While wanting to live happily ever after

But this struggle

This trouble

It was a thorn in my side

I laugh so I don't cry

The thought of suicide

But the devil is a lie

I decide

Joy will drive

Drive me to a happy and peaceful place

Protecting my space

Negative people and energy will stop at the gate

I smile again and again

Laughter is now my friend

Precious Memories

Remembering the things that hurt me

Painful memories

That stayed with me

It had me feeling a certain type of way

Fast food restaurant

Young lady couldn't understand what I said

Wishing at that moment, I was dead

Stuttering messing with my head

Why couldn't someone else deal with this instead

Indeed, Precious Memories

Name Called

Nowhere in sight

Running for my life

Failure to speak leads to lies

A smile on my face

Dying on the inside

Precious memories

What so precious about these memories

Seeing the many faces looking at you while you speak

Many looking at you funny

Like I'm retarded, a dummy

These memories

So precious to me

Because now I'm free

Free from what people think of me

Helping others who have been down this road like me

Looking to heal many

That will indeed be precious memories

The Thoughts in My Head

The thoughts in my head

Suicidal thoughts

Hurt by the words they said

Talk straight

Retarded boy

Speech impediment took away my joy

Hard to make a joyful noise

The thoughts in my head

Doing my best to be spirit-led

The painful memories

So many tears shed

Why was I born this way?

Why was I chosen to deal with this pain?

When will this change?

Hard not to complain

When they look at you, strange

Speech therapy

The thought of it made me angry

Trying to teach me how to speak slowly

The frustration and aggravation

Fighting to release my tension

Childhood to adulthood Fighting the thoughts in my head

God steps in

I no longer care what people think and what they said

You Are Not Crazy

You are not crazy

To dream how you dream

No matter how hard it seems

They don't see what you see

Your losing sleep

Trying to be the best you can be

It's not easy

While trying to balance everything

Lack of support

Feeling like you're drowning

You're not crazy

You think differently

Many think you're out of your mind

They don't see the grind

They don't know the time you put into your craft

Overcoming your past

Trying to be the head of your class

Trying not to let procrastination get the best of you

Trying not to become lazy

You'll accomplish all you set out to do

You're not crazy

<u>The Voices in My Head</u>

I keep hearing these voices in my head

Saying that you're better off dead

Wounded by the words they said

Trying to be free from their curse

Yes words hurt

Trying to move forward with my life

Trying to live a better life

But I'm in a mental fight

Making a conscious decision

Renewing my mind daily

I need my mind free

Free from the voices in my head

I no longer care what they said

Better off alive, not dead

I'm looking ahead

Inspired by the tears shed

I'm not called to be the tail

I'm called to be the head

Positivity now fills my head

I'm worthless

I'm useless

Nothing good is going to come out of my life

All my life, I had to fight

I'm tired of complaining

Tired of maintaining

Some things I'm changing

New heights I'm gaining

Trying to escape my negative thinking

I found myself sinking

Changing my surrounding

I now call myself worthy

I am valuable

I now speak positive words over me

Stuck

Stuck in the same place

Wondering when God will help you out of your rut

Stuck,

Wanting change

Trying not to complain

A new life

A new day

A new place

Stuck,

Stuck in the same place

Barely making it

I don't know how much more you can take

You don't want to die here

There is so much you want to share

You question why you're here

Tired of the struggle and the trouble

Wondering when will the sunshine

Stuck

All you see is a dark cloud over you

Wanting to get people to notice you

Notice who you are

So, you can go far

Stuck,

Crying out for help

You don't know what else to do

There's so much you want to do

You don't have the resources or finances to do it

So, you stay stuck in the same place

Settle at this place

Trying to make it through another day

Barely making it

With a smile on your face

But you know you're faking it

Wanting so much more

Wanting an open door

Knowing in your heart that you're better than this

You were created for more than this

Stuck in the same place

God help me get out of this place

Positive Thinking

Positive thinking was something I didn't do much when I was dealing with the hurt and pain of my past. I dwelled too much on what I experience. Why think positively, knowing that stuttering will be stuck with me for the rest of my life? I kept quiet most times, so I didn't have to speak. It became the norm for me. I didn't make many friends growing up because I stayed to myself. I didn't want to open myself up to being laughed at or made fun of. I felt the best thing for me to do at that time, was to shut up and kept to myself. I resorted to fighting as my way of defending myself growing up. If somebody laughs or makes fun of me, I will take care of them my way. My method was fighting. I got so tired of the suffering. I felt fighting was my way of releasing all my anger toward the people who called me names and thought I was retarded. I didn't know anything positive would come out of my life dealing with a speech impediment. I had low self-esteem. I didn't think highly of myself to even think positively. I was living a defeated life. I didn't allow God to transform my mind and my thinking. I was too busy thinking negatively. There were many times in school I would be asked to read, and even before reading, I already saw myself stuttering and messing up. I would do everything possible to avoid reading or speaking. I would ask to go to the bathroom so my name was not called, or if they are reading in a circle, I would ask to leave before it is my turn. I saw defeat even before trying. Are you feeling defeated today? Have you already counted yourself out because you don't think you can do it? I would avoid anything that had to do with speaking in front of people. If I had to do something in the church, I would make sure I was not there or find an excuse. It became a cycle for me. I wasn't thinking positively. I allowed fear to torment and consumed me. I made fear sit on my throne and rule and reign. I allowed fear to run my life.

I had to make up my mind to change my thinking. **Starve the fear and feed my faith** which I will speak on later in this book. I had to learn that without positive thinking, I won't get anywhere in life. Positive thinking should lead you to action. A made-up mind is the first step to doing great things. If you don't decide in your mind that you will do something significant, it will never get done. That goes for even negative thinking. So many people are imprisoned because of negative thinking and choices. They decided to hurt or harm someone, and their consequence was imprisonment. You have a choice to either think positive or negative. Either one you choose has a consequence. We are all trying to live a good life. We want great things for ourselves and our families. We want to be able to enjoy nice things. Our motivation each day is to go out and do what we can to get those things. We can't accomplish this without being positive. We can't do it without being in our right mind. We must purpose in our hearts and mind that nothing or no one will interfere with our focus. We are all on a mission to do something great in life.

We are determined to do whatever it takes to make it. We can't allow our past to hinder the future. People are waiting to be touched and changed by your gift.

Key Points

You won't go far without positive thinking.

Positive thinking will get you through difficult times.

Surround yourself with positive thinkers.

Suggestions for Positivity

Wake up every day looking to do positive things.

Think of good things that make you happy.

Don't leave room for negative thoughts to come in.

Prayer

Father, I pray for those who are in trouble in their mind today. I pray, Holy Spirit, you arrest their mind. I pray for those who are tormented by their past and their losing sleep because of it. I pray you give them peaceful sleep going forward. I pray for those who are worried about their tomorrow and help them to enjoy today. I pray for those who are troubled in their spirit and can't seem to rest. I pray for rest. May they rest in you. I pray for those surrounded by toxic people who have nothing positive or good to say. I pray you will free them from those people. Put them in the right environment. I pray for their protection today. May they live a peaceful life. In Jesus' Name, Amen.

Positive Thinking

Trying to change my stinking thinking

Trying to keep my head above water

Realizing that I'm sinking

I'm taking a beating

Because of my thinking

You see a smile on my face

Looks can be deceiving

Dealing with things internally

Feeling like this walk is lonely

I had to renew my mind

Wasting valuable time

Peace is now mine

Failing to complete my mission would be a crime

Now my mind is in line

Positive thinking, preaching those who want my time

Speaking words of life

To all those who lie and say they're fine

No more losing

I now have positive thinking

Now I'm winning

You Can't Think Straight

You can't think straight

So many things aren't going your way

Some things delay

You're heartbroken again

Losing friends

You can't think straight

So much time you waste

Needing healing today

Trying to pray these things away

Thinking of therapy today

But you don't want to let a stranger in

Not realizing if you don't

The healing won't begin

You fight your issues

Wrestling with evil thoughts

Also afraid of therapy

Too focus on the cost

You can't think straight

Seek help today

Before it's too late

Running Out of Time

I feel like I'm running out of time

I got a lot on my mind

Pretending I'm fine

Trying to get my life back inline

Dealing with some cloudy days

The sun refuses to shine

Trying to accomplish so much

Trying not to give up

Fighting the negative thinking

Trying to keep my head above water

Trying to get my life in order

Questioning who on my team

Who can speak life into me?

Who can see my reality?

My time is running

The Lord is coming

Trying to live my dreams

But I've been stagnant lately

Trying not to have my gift end up in the cemetery

Father, forgive me for wasting time

Help my mind

I don't want to run out of time

Preacher's Kid

It is one thing to deal with stuttering. It's another thing to be a preacher's kid. Combine these two and imagine what it's like. I tried to avoid the spotlight already because of stuttering, but I was born into being a preacher's kid. No running from it. You are constantly watched, and all eyes are on you. You got to live and behave a certain way. The choices you make affect the family, especially your parents. **Talk about being even quieter.** You don't have to be a preacher's kid, but maybe your mom or dad is in the public eye and holds a prominent position. This impacts the child or children, and they must act accordingly. You're forced to watch everything you say or do because you have an image to protect. I'm already dealing with enough as a person dealing with his speech; I didn't need that problem, at least that problem I can avoid. Preacher's kid who stutters and is asked to do certain things but avoids them because I genuinely didn't have enough faith in God.

As I said earlier, I allowed God to touch one area of my life but didn't allow him to touch the sensitive area of my life. This was a sensitive area for me. I didn't like to pray because it involved talking. I didn't want to talk because I didn't want to stutter. I did my best not to be around at prayer meetings or any kind of function or event involving me talking. I'm not saying that being a preacher's kid is terrible at all, but because of the issue I am dealing with it became a struggle. I had to realize that I had to live my own life for God despite who my father was. I must live, laugh, and love life even as a preacher kid with a speech barrier.

Feed Your Faith, Starve Your Fear. Looking back, I realize I fed my fear and starved my faith. I allowed fear to torment me. I allowed fear to cripple me. I wore fear all over me. I had embraced fear, and I didn't want to let go. I grew up in church. The church is in me. I knew all about faith. I knew all about walking by faith and not by sight (2 Corinthians 5:7, NJKV) or faith is the substance of things hoped for and the evidence of things not seen (Hebrews 11:1, NJKV). I knew about faith, but I let fear overpower my faith. I allow fear to control my life. I allowed it to control me in school. When I had to give a speech or presentation, I ran from the challenge. I made sure I was nowhere around when my name was called, or I made up an excuse. I lied, ran, and did everything possible to be free from speaking. Anytime I was asked to do something in school or church, fear would come over me because I didn't let go of the pain of yesterday. Yesterday's pain can hinder the things you want to accomplish today. Fear came because my mind was full of hurtful memories or situations I let sit. Carrying around hurt and pain is no good for you. No good for your health. No good for all you want to accomplish in life. There is so muc' in you to do. Don't carry the pain of yesterday with you today. Be free. Feeding your faith every day is necessary for your focus. Believing that you can do all things you put your mind to do. You can't accomplish anything until you have decided that you can. Faith it to make it. What are you fearful about? What is troubling your mind? Are you worrying yourself sick? How do you see yourself is the question I had to ask myself. I want to do great things but can't do it if I don't operate in faith instead of fear. We operate in faith every day, and we don't realize it. We believe by faith to wake up each day. We believe by faith to get to and from wherever we go daily. We schedule trips, we plan events by faith, hoping to get to that day. We have faith in some areas of our lives, but when it comes to something complex, faith is gone. Faith is nowhere present. We want God to touch one area of our lives but leave the other area alone. I'm guilty of this. Until we let God be in charge, we will be better off. We can say that positive thinking=Faith and negative thinking=Fear. Negative thinking can contribute to fear. Positive thinking can contribute to faith. Faith is what is going to help you to overcome any obstacle in your way, along with positive thinking.

<u>Key Points</u>

You can't choose where and how you were born

There is greatness in you regardless of your circumstance

You have to faith it to make it

Faith sometimes will be the only thing you have left

Fear can cripple or paralyze you

Fear robs you of joy, peace, and happiness

Suggestions for Daily Encouragement

Share your painful story, and it will help somebody

Give your issue to God and leave it there

Don't hold yourself back

Speak words of life to yourself daily.

Feed your mind with positive thoughts

Surround yourself with encouragers, motivators

Prayer

I pray for every preacher kid today. I pray for those who wish they weren't preacher kid. You didn't ask to be one, but you are dealing with it. Your tired. Frustrated and want to live a normal life. You question why I was born into this. Father, I pray you remind them that you have a purpose and plan for all things. Touch those preacher kids who had it rough. Who was force or try to be someone they're not. Touch those dealing with identity crisis. Many don't know who they are without being a preacher kid. Touch those who had to live with secrets. Touch those who had to hide. Touch those who had to deal with things too heavy to carry' I pray for healing of their mind, heart, and spirit. Remind them that you have a plan for their lives. Touch those who left the church due to so many wrongdoings. Touch those dealing with church hurt. I pray you return the prodigal son and daughter back home for you're not through with them yet in Jesus' name amen.

Preacher kid

Born into this

There is no hiding

I can't run from this

This stuttering kid

Prayed God take away this

This cross is too heavy

Too much to bear

I cried many tears

Question many times why I'm here

This preacher kid

Loving behind the scenes

Doing my best not to be seen

Leaving my gifts behind me

Don't want my gift to expose me

This preacher kid

Had to search within

My purpose is much bigger than me

What inside of me is someone healing

Realizing it's not about me

Stuttering preacher kid

Sharing my story

Sharing is my healing

My story is for his glory

Lost in the church

Lost in the church

Trying to find my way

I do church work

I try to sing and pray

But my mind is elsewhere

I can't concentrate

My mind is on the girl I was with the night before

Trying to worship the lord

My mind is focused on leaving out the church door

My relationship with God needs fixing

I know my spiritual condition

I need a check-up

I need an evaluation

Something wrong

So many things got my attention

So many distractions

So many things I allow in my path

That causes my relationship

My friendship with the one who calls me a friend

Goes down the hill

Speaking out of my mouth

Saying I want his will

But no time to hear his will

Focus on other things

The girls

The things of this world

Has all my time

But I find

My life is out of line

Having to cut off some people

Change some things

Trying to find my way back

Trying to get back on track

Doing church work

But lost in the church

Dying Slowly

Dying slowly

The cancer of unforgiveness

Is taking its toll on me

Spreading all through my bloodstream

It has its way with me

Unhappy and unstoppable

Feeling sick and uncomfortable

Bound and no cure is found

Feeling weak

The poison is destroying me

No longer feel free

Wanting to release

Release all the hatred feeling

My emotions need healing

Dying slowly

Remembering the one who hurt me

Now feeling angry

Flashback, Memories

Wanting to be free

Wanting to be healthy again

Is there a cure for my disease

Dying slowly

My time

My time

When will it be my time

Lord, am I next in line

Am I even on your mind

When will happiness enter my life

My time

When will I become a husband or wife

When will everything in my life go right

When will everything go according to my plan

Lord, you must understand

I am a great woman

I am a great man

My time

When will it be my time to shine

When will my storm end

When will there be sunshine

Lord, there must be a reason

Why isn't it my season

My season of joy, laughter, happiness

Why am I in distress

Why am I going through

Why is my life a mess

Lord, you know what is going on in my mind

I am wondering

When will it be my time

Feed Your Faith & Starve Your Fears

For many years

I fed my fear and starved my faith

I allowed fear to have its way

It got in the way

Didn't want to pray

A fight every day

To say what I want to say

I had words

Pronouns, verbs, proverbs

I wanted to pronounce

I couldn't otter

Afraid I would stutter

Fear kept me quiet

Fear kept me paralyzed

I finally realize

How much time do I waste?

Feeding my fear

Starving my faith

Comfort Zone

My comfort zone was being alone, closed in, and remaining quiet. I didn't make many friends growing up besides my church friends. My comfort zone protected me from hurt and pain. It was easy to stay in a place where I didn't have to speak. I avoided any kind of interaction as much as I could. My comfort zone kept me out of trouble. Growing up, I had to defend myself from bullies who sought to embarrass and make fun of my speech. Getting violent was my way of releasing my frustration and anger. Many tried to pull me out of my comfort zone by making me must speak. One way or another, I did my best to avoid it, even if it meant not showing up or being around. My comfort zone was my peaceful place. I didn't realize that it would hurt me later. Stepping out of your comfort zone is a huge factor. I didn't want to take it because I knew what comes with it. It involves communication. I didn't push myself to do anything great because it would mean I would have to talk. I would have to get in front of people. The thought of large crowds or talking to people I didn't know was terrifying, and I did want to face that. I did my best to avoid it. I had to learn that to do anything significant required killing your comfort zone. You can't grow or achieve anything in life if you don't step out of what you used to. Growing up, I didn't want to hear that. I was comfortable where I was. Until this speech issue goes away, I will stay right where I was comfortable was my thinking. I had to realize that I was holding myself back from embracing a wonderful future with the goals and dreams I had in mind. Have you ever had goals and dreams beyond this world but felt hopeless? Feeling helpless? Feeling cripple? You can see the finish line but don't know how you will get there. Don't know how you will get over this hurdle? Why won't this sickness, this disease, this trouble, this struggle, this disappointment, this failure just go away? In my comfort zone, I stay connected to the familiar. Stay connected with people who already knew me. Who already knew my issue? I was very skeptical about who I was around because I was carrying the memories of the past with me wherever I went and anyone who sought to make me their laughingstock. I remembered the feeling of shame and hurt. So, to avoid that from happening, into my comfort zone I went. A part of me wanted to make friends, and a part of me didn't. No one wants to feel alone or lonely, but I choose alone rather than be hurt by words and laughter from someone who didn't truly know me. I was fearful of leaving my comfort zone because it meant I had to take a step out into the unknown. Not knowing what to expect from people when I decide to speak. I had to learn to take a risk. Learn to get out of this comfort zone I put myself in. Connecting with people is essential because you don't know how much a connection can be beneficial to you. I had to get out of my negative thinking. I had so many negative thoughts that it was sickening. I have now remained in a positive mindset because I spent so many years thinking negatively. I am much stronger now. Coming out of my comfort zone is necessary to achieve everything ahead of me.

Go Afraid. There were times in my life when I didn't want to try anything because I was too afraid. I didn't think too highly of myself. Low self-esteem got the best of me. I cared too much about what people thought. It got the best of me. I was always counting or naming all the negative reasons I shouldn't move forward. All the negative feelings of being too afraid to jump. Too afraid to find out that you can land where you need to be when you jump. The one thing I learn, and I hope you get this, is that the fear doesn't go away when going for something new. It's ok to be nervous. It's ok to go into unfamiliar territory not knowing what will happen. Go afraid. Don't be afraid to jump. Don't be afraid to take that leap of faith. You don't know what is waiting for you on the other side. Go afraid.

Kryptonite. When I took a GOD look at myself, I learned I was my kryptonite. You can be your own worst enemy. You can hold yourself back by not trusting God. Sometimes even people can be your kryptonite. They suck you dry. They drain all your energy. They don't want to see you elevate past them. They're ok with everything being even. Sometimes we can waste so many years or time holding ourselves back. Whatever you are holding on to, past hurt or pain, whatever your kryptonite is, don't let it kill your hope. Don't let it destroy your dream.

Key Points

You can't do anything great staying in your comfort zone

Comfort zone is acceptable if your plans are to do and be nothing.

Leaving your comfort zone isn't easy, but necessary for your growth

Suggestions out of Your Comfort Zone

Step out and go after what you want

Connect with people who've accomplished where you're trying to go

Set higher goals that are beyond your comfort zone

Prayer

I pray for those too afraid to leave their comfort zone. I pray you strengthen their faith today to walk out on the water. Remind them father that you are with them wherever they go. I pray for their ideas. I pray that you will connect them with the right people, the right resources to go in the direction of success. I pray for boldness. I pray for the mind. I pray you remove self-doubt and fear. I pray that they will encourage themselves to step up and step out and accomplish all that they envision in Jesus' name amen.

Comfort Zone

I don't want to leave home

Afraid to talk on the phone

Fear that I will end up alone

Comfort zone

Leaving the pain behind

Trying to chase after the prize

With so little time

I got work to do

Trying to make some moves

I'm free

I'm free to be me

Speak how I want to speak

No longer feeling weak

Fear no longer has control of me

Packing my bag, leaving my comfort zone

Never to return

That place is no longer my home

<u>There's More to My Story</u>

There's more to my story

Having to share

This is for his glory

The things I will share

You will not believe

You may look at me differently

Look at me funny

But please don't judge me

God is working inside of me

He's making me clean

Sharing my story

I choose to expose me

My struggles and troubles

Will bring healing to many

So, I sacrifice myself

For his glory

Stay tuned

There's more to my story

My flesh is weak

Allow my feelings to get the best of me

Going after what I want

While telling God to excuse me

Using my gift

To satisfy me

Asking God later to forgive me

Mishandling

Mistreating

Misleading

Deceiving

Just to make myself happy

But in the end

I feel lonely

Enjoying the girl's time

Living the dream

Now back to reality

They aren't for me

Now having to break free

But they become attached to me

Now trying to flee

Stop texting

They are wondering what happen to me

Why the sudden change

Why you won't talk to me

Afraid to say this was just temporary

Needing you only for a season

I already had a good reason

Reason to leave

You aren't God's will for me

Leaving them broken

Made them feel like they were chosen

Insecurity

Ignoring the voice of God completely

Not wanting to wait

Want to have a good time

These girls are fine

Wanting God to change his mind

I recognize something is wrong with me

I needed fixing

My flesh is weak

Despite all, I have done

He still talks to me

Try Love Again

Growing up, I didn't think I would ever find love. I didn't know any female would accept me. I dealt with low self-esteem for so long that I didn't believe I was worthy of being loved or receiving it. I didn't talk to any girls besides the ones that were at church. It was much easier to deal with them because they already knew me. I didn't want to meet anybody new because of the fear of rejection. I often wondered who would want to be with someone with a disability for the rest of their lives. Although I knew how to love, I was fearful. I had to learn that there are people who don't care about your disability, your struggle, or your trouble; they accept you for who you are because there is so much more to you than your flaws and issues. I had to learn also that people watch you; they observe how you move and carry yourself. I believe because of how I conducted myself; I was able to be in a relationship and find love. I held on to relationships because of the fear of starting over. I didn't want to keep starting over. I didn't want someone to have to learn that I stutter versus dealing with someone who already knew that I did and accepted me anyway. Starting over is never easy. All the hard work you put into a relationship, only for it to fail, is not a good feeling. It is not easy for people who stutter or have a disability or a physical ailment to find love or start over. There is a lot that goes with it. You first must deal with yourself. Deal with your insecurities to even look or seek out a potential mate. You must be mentally and emotionally ready to deal with someone. You must see the bigger picture. You can't date just to date; there must be a purpose for it.

For me, I found it easier to begin as friends. In friendship, you get to learn and ask all the necessary questions and spend time getting to know each other to see if the person is someone you can have a future with. You save yourself the unnecessary heartache or headache by just being friends. I have learned not to rush things. Rushing things lead to problems. I also found that God had no voice or say in my decisions, which was an even bigger problem. I wanted God's stamp of approval, his blessing, but I was too busy doing my own thing. I didn't give God my time so he could direct me in choosing a relationship. I held on to people who God was clearly saying let go, but because I was afraid to start over, I continued to stay until I had to let go. I didn't give God my issue, problem, worry, or fear. I held on to all of them and carried them with me. That can be a problem because you can hurt someone when you are not where you need to be. You hurt the mate you're seeing because you both agreed to be in a relationship, but now you must pull away because it's not the right time or the relationship isn't for you. I would have saved my heartache and headache if I didn't lean on my understanding. If I only allowed God to direct my path, things would be different. Trying to love again. After you are stronger, wiser, and better, try love again. Most of all, prayer is key. Make God the center of all decisions.

Key Points

Don't try love again until you're emotionally and mentally ready

Don't be afraid to date

Put God first in all decisions

Suggestions For Loving You

More prayer. Being with the wrong person can ruin your life

Take yourself out and treat yourself

Show yourself friendly

Prayer

I pray for those too afraid to try love again. So many have failed in this area and they're tired. So many are tired of giving their heart to people and be mistreated. So many are frustrated with dating. So many are tired of wasting their time. I pray you will lead them to what is right. Help them to make right choices. May they be led by your spirit in this area. May they be able to discern that is right and wrong. Protect their heart from intruders with bad motives and agendas. Touch those who need healing. May they date when their heart is ready. Take control today. In Jesus' Name Amen.

Try love again

I don't think I want to

That won't be a winning move

I already lose

Dealing with some issues

I would be a fool

To bring a girl into my world

That wouldn't be the right thing to do

So, I take this time

To renew my mind

Allow God to do work on the inside

Inside of me

He is healing me

Preparing me

For what he has for me

It will be heaven sent

I will then try love again

A Kiss

A kiss causes a soul tie

Causing so many things to bind

Bind together

A connection

A heart-to-heart connection

Time and mind collide

A kiss connects with the soul

Your heart is beating out of control

A kiss causes your spirit to leap

Feelings rise

Possibly stirring up your sex drive

A kiss can make you come alive

A kiss ignites a fire

Burning desire

You are feeling the burn

Feeling the heat

A kiss can make you weak

Causing you to lose sleep

Can't keep your eyes closed

The kiss touches your soul

Trying to have self-control

Trying to keep yourself together

Wondering if it is too late to be made whole

A kiss changes your direction

Causing you to be speechless

Helpless

Not knowing what to do with yourself

Unity

Unity of the mind

The soul and the spirit

You feel the rush

You question if it is love or lust

Now feeling some type of way

Thinking about the person all-day

Memory, flashback

Leaving you in a daze

Unable to speak

Unable to think about anything else

Wondering if you're in a dream

Saying to yourself, is there something wrong with me

A kiss opens the door

Leaving you wanting more

A kiss

Some want it

Some wait for it

Some are waiting for the perfect day

Some are waiting for their wedding day

A kiss you will remember for the rest of your life

The greatest kiss is between the groom and bride

Holding hands, looking into each other eyes

A kiss is more beautiful when it's husband and wife.

You Can't Think Straight

You can't think straight

So many things aren't going your way

Some things delay

You're heartbroken again

Losing friends

You can't think straight

So much time you waste

Needing healing today

Trying to pray these things away

Thinking of therapy today

But you don't want to let a stranger in

Not realizing if you don't

The healing won't begin

You fight your issues

Wrestling with evil thoughts

Also afraid of therapy

Too focus on the cost

You can't think straight

Seek help today

Before it's too late

I'm Your Slave

I'm your slave

Hypnotize

Mesmerize by your walk

Your body

Your talk

You have my heart captive

You're more than attractive

Lock in your prison

You took my vision

Now wondering if I have made the right decision

Bound

You have a strong hold on me

Giving up on yourself is not easy

Because my mind is not free

My mind is stuck in your penitentiary

I'm your slave

My heart, I gave away

You're in control

I'm your slave

You have my heart and soul

Trying to break free

I'm ready for battle

I will have the victory

Distracted Because You're Attractive

Distracted because you're attractive

Lock in your prison

Holding me captive

With your looks

Your body

Knowing there is more to you

You're somebody

Distracted because you're attractive

Can't concentrate

Wanting to see your face

Only interested in the physical

Don't care about your mental, emotional, and spiritual

I just want what I want

Go my way

Enjoy today

Then keep you in the past, like yesterday

Tomorrow wanting nothing to do with you

You can say I use you

To satisfy my own needs

But I'm still not happy

Distracted because you're attractive

When I'm ready

I want to see you again

Wanting to get to know me

But all I want to get to know is your body

Can't shake the thought of you

I don't love you

But I lust you

Don't want to be free

Enjoying my time in your penitentiary

But now, back to reality

Realizing you're not good for me

So, I search for a way out of your prison

No longer wanting to be held captive

I'm distracted because you're attractive

I Will Remember You

I will remember you

Remember the first time I laid eyes on you

You've got my attention

Wanted you to come in my direction

Seeking plotting in my mind

How will I get a moment of your time

I knew one day you would be connected to me in some way

I can't believe the day

You got my attention

You and me

Poetry

Connected you and me

The rest is history

Still in awe

Still in disbelief

Never thought there would be a you and me

Sometimes wondering is this a dream

Realizing this is reality

You reveal that you are more than fine

You affect my mind

A pure giver

Able to deliver

Deliver all that is needed to make a man happy

Treating him so well, he can't wait to see you

I will remember you

As you prepare to leave

Wishing that was a dream

But it's reality

Afraid To See You

Afraid to see you

Afraid to look into your eyes and want you

Afraid of what I will do

When I'm alone with you

Don't want to stay away

Wondering if I need to

So I don't feel any more pain

Afraid to see you

Afraid my feelings will come alive again

Afraid to tell you

I want to be more than your friend

Afraid of going back down that road with you again

Enjoying the ride

Knowing it will soon end

Afraid to be lost in your love

Lost in your kiss

Lost in your hug

Afraid to see you

Afraid to see your smile

Afraid of saying I love you

I know it's been a while

Afraid of missing you

Afraid that our love will fade away

Afraid that things will change

Afraid of moving on

Afraid I'm weak

Afraid I'm not strong

Afraid to see you

Afraid of living without you

Till We Meet Again

Till we meet again

Till we see each other face to face

Waiting to see your smile again

That will make my day

Till we meet again

Till we meet at that special place

To feel your warm embrace

Speechless

No words to say

Till we meet again

Wiping the tears from your face

We have come a long way

We are finally here

Full of laughter and cheer

Not wanting to say goodbye

Having so much fun

Time flew on by

Tears fall again

The day is ending

Not wanting to let go

Time to go our separate ways

Wishing our time together didn't have to end

Lover to lover

Friend to friend

Till we meet again

Fooling Myself

Fooling myself

Thought I could move on

Thought I could love someone else

Trying to get you out of my mind

But that was a waste of time

Dealing with myself

Checking myself

Realizing I needed help

Fooling myself

Thinking I could get rid of the thought of you

Telling myself

That I don't love and care about you

Heartbreak

When you find someone else

Fooling myself

You can't hear my cry for help

I don't want anyone else

The hurt and pain my heart felt

When I see you loving someone else

Needing time away

To heal and get help

Not ready to move on

Fooling myself

Tearing Down Your Walls

Tearing down your walls

Piece by piece

Brick by brick

Until your heart, I see

The power of my words

Causing you to believe in me

Seeing the bricks falling in front of me

You will look into my eyes

You will know I am for real

You will feel

Feel my heartbeat

Tearing down your walls

I'm like no other

I'm not like the last guy

I'm not like the last girl

I will change your world

A breath of fresh air

Knocking down your walls

I'm not going anywhere

Until your heart, I receive

Willing to sweat and bleed

Until you realize I'm not playing

I want to make you mine

Your walls won't stop me

I am patience

I'm willing to endure

The blood and sweat will pour

Due to the hard work I put in

I know change is going to come

Your walls aren't stronger than me

Your walls will fall like it did at Jericho

Tearing down your walls

Until I have your heart and soul

That's my goal

Avoiding You

Avoiding you

Doing my best not to see you

Trying not to think of you

But I lose that fight

You win the battle of my mind

My thoughts and feeling

You win it all, and having it all

Avoiding you

Mix feelings

Wanting to see you one minute

I don't want to see you the next

A battle between my spirit and my flesh

Wondering if you have a hold

A hold on me

A stronghold

But I will let this go

I will just avoid you

Until the thought of you leaves

Avoiding you

I won't allow you to have control of me

I will do what I must do

Back and forth

Wanting you close

The next minute wanting you to go away

Wondering why I feel this way

Avoiding you

I need time to think things through

<u>Tired Of Being the Other</u>

Tired of being the other

Tired of being the one that must be undercover

Having to hide all the time

Losing my mind

I'm really wasting my time

I'm not your top priority

Tired of second place

Tired of being treated this way

Tired of being the other

Tired of being put to the side

Tired of being deny

My feelings I must hide

But it ends here

I'm not going through another day

Another week, month, years

This will be over

I have cried my last tears

Time for you to make a choice

I will not lose my Joy

I'm doing what is best for me

I will release

We love each other

But I refuse to settle for the name other

A Beautiful Site To See

A beautiful sight to see

Staring at your beauty

Refusing to leave

You are one of the most beautiful things or people I have ever seen

I am just amazed

I am in a daze

Because you make me feel some type of way

I can't take my eyes off you

Wondering what I will do?

I refuse to leave you

I refuse to leave your presence

Trying to move on with my life

Act like I've never seen you

But that will be the biggest mistake of my life

Forget you even exist

I can't do this

I can't handle being away from you

I need you close to me

You're a beautiful sight to see

The Right One

The right one

Waiting for the right one to come along

Lord, why do I have to wait so long

Waiting for the right man or woman

Also afraid to take a chance

Don't want to get my heart broken again

Don't want to start over again

The right one

Wondering where he or she will come from

Wondering who God has made just for me

That special person to be a part of my destiny

The man or woman of my dreams

The right one

I want the real deal

Someone who is fulfilling God's will

Someone who wouldn't lie, cheat or steal

A real gentlemen

A real lady

I want the right one

The one who God created for me

Trying To Tempt Me

Trying to live the good life

Be faithful to my man or woman or husband or wife

Here comes distraction

Trouble comes entering in

Walking down the street

A stranger takes a peek at me

He or she likes what they see

Whisper, whistling rings in the street

Trying to get my attention

Wanting me to go in their direction

I won't give them the time of day

I already got what I want and need

What can you offer me

I am already happy

The enemy is trying to tempt me

Bringing an attractive person in front of me

Wanting me to cheat

Ruin my relationship or marriage

Ruin everything

But I smile and laugh

The enemy's objective won't come to pass

Don't Lead Me On

Don't lead me on

You've been playing around for so long

You flirt and say all the nice things

But I see the games you are playing

Wanting me to fall for you

So you do everything you can to win me over

The game is over

Don't lead me on

Don't play me

Don't use me

I am looking for someone who will appreciate me

Respect me

Treat me like royalty

Not someone only interested in having sex with me

I want someone who will treat me like a lady

Don't lead me on

Will you commit to me and only me

If not, then move on

I am tired of the games

I am looking to change my last name

I know what I want

I am strong

You will not waste my time

You will not lead me on

Painful Fragrance

Trying to get your fragrance out of my room

Trying to move on

But the smell lingers around

Trying to forget all that went wrong

Still feeling your touch

Still smelling your fragrance on me

Taking so many showers and it won't leave me

I can't forget your smell

Remembering the time I spend with you

Felt like hell

Holding me against my will

Without a care in the world

Still remembering you saying I am a beautiful girl

Until you hurt me

Changing my world

Turning my world upside down

The smell of a man turns my smile into a frown

Afraid to let another man into my space

Afraid things will end the same way

Trying to forget the way you made me feel

Need time to heal

Need time away

Away from everything

I need healing from your painful fragrance

I Don't Want to Go Down Memory Lane

It will lead me to hurt and pain

The pain of yesterday

Reliving everything again

I don't need to be reminded

Reminder of what I regret

Reminder of what I left

Memory lane

What do I gain

For going down that road again

Trying to forget the memory

Trying not to remember history

All I can think about is misery

The agony

All I can remember is being lonely

All I can remember is being abused

I refuse

I refuse to drive down memory lane

I want to smile again

I want to be happy again

Going to stay in the right lane

Not going down the road to hurt and pain

Not going down memory lane

I Can't Believe

Your smile I will no longer see

Wishing this was a dream

Your voice I will no longer hear

Wishing you were here

Hoping this wasn't reality

All I am left with is your memories

Memories

Your memories will keep me

When the days are long and lonely

I can't believe

You left so suddenly

Will need God to help me

Will need him to comfort me

Trying to hide the pain

Trying to hide the tears

Trying to handle the change

I will never see you again

I'm still in disbelief

Rest in peace

I'm left with your memories

I still can't believe

God, I need you to help me

I Would Be A Fool

I would be a fool to let you go

I chose to keep you in the friend zone

No feeling expressed or shown

I'm good at being alone

But your presence is captivating

My fire and desire for your go higher

Things are changing

You're constantly missed

But I go to do some explaining

Fear and insecurities

Tries to block my blessing

My low self-esteem took me in a different direction

Desiring your love, attention, and affection

Yes, I'm confessing my innermost thoughts

I wasn't trying to take the lost

Losing you would have been devastating

In the arms of someone else

My heart couldn't take it

I stepped up to let you know

Loving you forever is my goal

I would be a fool to let you go

Freedom

Don't Waste Your Pain. I felt growing up that this stuttering was a pain. I carried this pain for a long time because it wasn't going away. I would be stuck with this forever. I had to realize there must be another way to deal with this. Don't waste your pain is what came to mind. Whatever has hurt you or is hurting you, find a way to turn your issue into a positive. I began to volunteer at a place called SAY. The Stuttering Association for the Young is a national non-profit organization that provides summer camp, speech therapy, and creative expression. It empowers, educates, and supports young people who stutter and the world surrounding them. It was part of my healing to be a part of a program that understands. This organization is a place of no judgment, love, acceptance, and freedom. It was the best place to be yourself. This place builds confidence in you and inspires you to do great things. Don't waste your pain. Your healing sometimes comes through sharing with others. I had to realize that I had something to give to this world. The key thing is turning your pain into power.

Give To Yourself. We often forget to give to ourselves. If you're like me, you will give your all to something or someone in need, or you just simply care what people deal with. That can be a good thing and a bad thing. Good thing because it shows that you care and does your heart go to give to something or someone worthy to receive.

The flip side is that you can give and give, and when it's time to give to yourself, you have nothing left. Sometimes that can leave you frustrated because you look to receive from those you've provided. I have learned that you're blessing sometimes doesn't come from those you give; it comes in different ways. I also learned you couldn't expect people to be like you. What I mean is don't expect you in other people. People will not have a heart like yours and give like you. You think differently. I had to learn to do everything and give unto the glory of God. Try not to concentrate on people not doing right by you when you're in need. One of the painful things is that you can give so much, and people would gladly take and take from you and never make a deposit in you. So many will withdraw from you and suck you dry, leaving you hopeless and helpless, and go along their merry way and not look back. Pay attention to your givers and takers. There are many ways to give. It doesn't have to be money. Some things are more valuable than money. Some people don't have the means to give, but they can offer their time, attention, prayer, etc. Give to yourself. Don't forget who is important that is you. Sometimes you must be selfish. Add no to your vocabulary if you haven't already. Say no so you don't have to deal with the consequences of saying yes. Be careful of what you say yes to. You might be paying a high price for your yes.

Give to yourself. Give to what matters to you. Sow into what you want to do in your life. We all have a gift or talent that can be used.

Invest in yourself. Do what you love to do. Ask yourself this question. What is something that you like to do that can create wealth for you? Think about it. Do you want to go back to school? Do you want to start a business? Do you want to go on vacation? Buy a house? A car? Give to yourself and make no apology for it. When you give and give, no one can tell you anything when you decide to give to yourself. I also had to learn to balance. I'm still learning to use wisdom and discernment in this area because I love helping people, but you can't help everyone. You can't be everyone's savior. There is only one savior, and that is Jesus Christ. In order to give to yourself, take wisdom and discernment with you. You'll need it. I believe in sowing seeds into something or someone, especially if you believe in the cause. You know that God will honor your love, gift, and sacrifice you make. God loves a cheerful giver. It does the heart good to give. I want to also to watch those around you when you start giving to yourself. When you decide to put your energy and effort into what you want to do, pay attention to your friends and family. Watch how they behave; watch how they react. You may lose some people when you start giving to yourself. Some people are selfish. Some people only think about themselves; me, myself, and I. Beware of those kinds of people. Beware of people who only contact you when they need a favor or need something. After you're done giving to them, meeting their needs, they're nowhere to be found. You've to be ok with losing people at this time of your life.

Surround yourself with givers. Surround yourself with those who pour into you and make deposits into you. Begin today to choose yourself. Do the things that make you happy. Do the things that put a smile on your face.

Make up in your mind that you won't neglect yourself ever again. There is so much in you that needs to come out of you. Allow God to do what is needed to be done in you. Giving to yourself also mean separation or isolation from the familiar. You may have to shut down your social media. Go on a fast. You may have to go away to a place to refresh, recharge, and rejuvenate. Do whatever it takes to better yourself, to better your life. Some of you've given a long time. It's time to reap what you have sown. It's time to live your best life. It's time to live for you. Make the necessary adjustments. Don't procrastinate, and don't let anyone talk to you out of what you truly deserve.

Key Points

Your pain will heal others.

Turn your pain into power.

God can use your pain.

Suggestions for Helping

Create something positive out of your pain.

Talk about your pain. It's part of your healing process.

Volunteer. Give your time somewhere. There is also healing in that.

Prayer

Father God, I pray for those who need peace and freedom today. So many are bound by so many things. So many are trying to fight their way through some things. I pray you break the shackles. I pray you lose them from strongholds today. I pray you help those dealing with so much in their mind, home, work, school. Touch the weary today. I pray you help them to walk in freedom. We're free in you. We claim it and speak it today into existence. In Jesus' Name Amen.

Trying Not To Waste The Pain

I know if I stay focus

My pain can bring change

Battling through what hurt me

Knowing that there is a plan before me

Trying to see the bigger picture

I know God is with me

Positivity

Trying to let it run through my vein

Doing my best to walk differently

Talk differently

Wanting the pain to leave me

Wanting to be free

Doing what is necessary

My pain will bring change

I gave my pain to God

He won't waste my pain

Trying To Hide the Pain

Trying to hide the pain

Trying to handle the change

Trying to hold on to memories

Since we will never be together again

Trying not to lose my mind

Trying to hold back tears

Because you will no longer be near

No longer being able to hug you

No longer being able to kiss you

Trying to hide the pain

Refusing to get close to anyone again

They all leave in the end

Keeping to myself

Needing no one else

Refuse to ask for help

Deal with the pain alone

Home alone

Not answering text messages and phone

Trying to hide the pain

Don't want a piece of me to be taken again

Dying On the Inside

While smiling on the outside

Trying to hide feelings

Knowing I need healing

Pretending everything is ok

While I make it through each day

Trying to deal with the hurt and pain

The loss, the change

Dying on the inside

Affecting all areas of my life

Would have never thought you would leave my side

Leave my life

Slowly dying

But I'm still trying

Trying to be strong

Trying to move on

Still can't believe you're gone

Didn't want you to leave

Wishing things were like before

Which hurts even more

Being real on the inside

Faking it on the outside

Crying on the inside

A laughter on the outside

Dying on the inside

Give To Yourself

For many years I put myself on the shelf

Always willing to help

Always willing to lend a helping hand

Full of compassion

Doing everything I can

Looking to be a problem solver

Looking to ease troubled minds

Not realizing I neglected myself sometimes

Always looking to be the savior

When there is only one

I had to get myself together

Get my mind together

Give to myself

No longer feeling guilty

When I choose me

Hope

Wondering what I see

Will I receive

Wondering when that day will be

Hoping

Wondering what the future holds for me

Doing my best to believe

My present is too dark to see

Praying that things will be better

That's the faith that I have

Trying not to let it die

Wanting the promises of God

I know he will never lie

Hope is what I hold on to

That is what is keeping me

Wanting things to change all around me

I am a work in progress

Despite my past

Despite what I am facing in my present

I am hopeful for the future

Hoping everything will work for my good

Hope is all I got

Trying to rise from the bottom to the top

Hope is what helps me get through the day

Hoping things will change

Hope is my new name

Freedom

Let them go

Choosing you

Now trying to be whole

Having new goals

You need to be at ease

Your mind needs to be free

You're walking in the direction of destiny

You're walking into new territory

Let them go

You're looking to grow

Avoiding confusion

Avoiding negativity

You're free

No more living in captivity

Choosing to be happy

Choosing to live peacefully

You experience some highs and lows

Making a better decision this time

Letting some things and people go

I'm Finally Free

Freeing myself from the unnecessary

Unnecessary hurt and pain

Don't want to go through this again

Forgiving you for hurting me

Forgiveness is for me

I'm choosing to be free

I'm finally free

See that unforgiveness is hurting me

Like cancer, it's a disease

Spreading rapidly

Causing me to be sick

Did my best to move on

But can no longer handle this

I'm finally free

I'm choosing to be happy

Doing what is best for me

No longer bound

The weight of unforgiveness was putting me down

I'm finally free

Ready to receive all that God has for me

Refusing to allow unforgiveness to hold up my destiny

You're Not Over It!

Are you really over it

Why are you holding on to it

You forgive but do not forget

Not realizing your heart is still harden

Still bound and not free

Because you fail to relief

Release that person or thing to God

You have the nerves to ask why my life is so hard

You're not over it

It's in the back of your mind

Thinking about it all the time

Thinking about that person all the time

Saying your fine

You're not fine

You're not over it

Holding onto the hurt and pain

Keep bringing up the thing over and over again

When that person enters your space

A dirty look enters your face

Flashback, yes, the memory still lives

You remembered it like it happened yesterday

You really haven't forgive

You're not over it

Quarantine

This quarantine

Revealing people reality

Having people panicking

Lives vanishing

Coronavirus

Bring the world to its knees

Lockdown

Wanting to be free

Quarantine

People afraid for their health

Hitting people pockets

Taking away people's wealth

Anxiety

Wondering will you face tomorrow

The world is in sorrow

Wondering what you will do

Rent due

Bills don't take a break

Many losing sleep

Many stay awake

All you can do is pray

Lord gives us a new day

Take the pain away

Online school

Kids adjusting to the new

Parents becoming teachers

Trying to do what they do

Their minds there're are trying not to lose

The testing of our faith

Coronavirus got us in our place

Working from home

Isolation

Some don't like being alone

Away from your church home

No more meeting

Having to resort to computer and phone

Quarantine

Is nothing like we have ever seen

Trust and believe

It is changing people's reality

It's waking us dead dreams

You are seeing creativity

Some things coming to life

Many are opening their eyes

Some receiving new life

Some seeing the light

Adjustment being made

But this quarantine won't go away

Until the people of God humble themselves and pray

Jericho

Dealing With My Jericho

Dealing with my Jericho

Round and round my wall

Will my wall fall with a shout?

Will everything come crashing down with my mouth?

 Will it bring me out?

I hear the voice of God saying

Will I be like Israel turning my journey into years?

Dealing with my Jericho

Remembering God saying he'll be with me

Wanting my wall to fall

But I have to surrender all

Even the things I like and love

God asking am I be willing to give it all up

Dealing with my Jericho

Will I let go?

Will I allow God to break down my wall?

Will I answer the call?

Will I surrender all?

Jericho, will I die at this place?

Will I say yes to God?

Will I see my wall break?

Depart From Me

Depart from me

Trying to live right so I don't hear those words

But I have fallen

I have made some mistakes

Trying to get my life straight

This walk is not easy

I have grown up in church

I know about the lord

But I have strayed away

I have a bible in my home

I know how to pray

But the world sucks me right in

Left church because it was boring

Church is not for me

I tried everything

Like drugs and sex, just to name a few

I'm surprised I'm still alive

So many times, I could have died

But I constantly hear God's voice

His voice telling me to come home

Right now, I feel empty

I feel alone

Even when doing the wrong things

I knew he was with me

Especially the night when that bullet misses me

Depart from me

Now trying to live right

Wanting God to welcome me

Welcome me back home

Back to where I used to be

Throwing away the weed

I know I need thee

Tired of running

Wanting to work for the lord

So, I can hear well done rather than depart from me

<u>Chosen</u>

Why did you choose me?

Why did you choose me to carry this thing?

I know I said God use me

But I didn't know I would have to deal with negativity

Deal with cruelty

Dealing with hurt and pain

Feel what I experience

Did you know beforehand I would make a difference?

Why did you choose me?

Choose me to go through the valley

What are you doing with me?

Why me

Why the suffering

Why did you choose this road for me?

Is it all for your glory?

Is this part of my journey

Is this part of my life story

Please explain to me

Why I have experienced the agony

Is it because you want me to feel what you felt?

Felt on the cross

Lord, I am lost

Trying to find my way

Trying to hear what you say

But why did you choose me

Why did you choose to use me?

Then I hear you say

This is all for my glory

Survival

I will survive this

I can handle this

Despite what happened in court

Despite the doctor's report

I will survive this

I am stronger than this

I have been through worse than this

I'm not going through it alone

God has been with me

Keeping his promise

Never leaving me

Never forsaking me

Going through my crisis

He reminds me that it is Christ Is

He is able to help me through financial difficulty

He is able to protect me when my enemies try to kill me

I will survive this

Going through some problems with my kids

I will survive this

Going through things with my family

I will get through this

Telling my problems about how big God is

I will survive this

I survive the hurt

I survive the pain

I survive the storm

I survive the shame

I am still here

I am still standing

I am still alive

No matter what it is

With God on my side

I will survive this

Critics

Ignore the critics

They aren't with it

They aren't with what you're trying to do

You have nothing to prove

Do what God tells you

They will always have something to say

When you pay attention to them

You delay your forward progress

You delay the process

They all saying negative things

Always complaining

Want you to stay where you are

Want to be comfortable

They don't want you to do greater things

Don't want you to be uncomfortable

Don't want you to be built

Your goals and dreams they trying to kill

Ignore your critics

Saying you can't do it

You can't handle it

But press forward and finish

Ignore the critics

Better

Trying to do the best I can

Trying to be a good father

Trying to be a provider

Trying to go higher

My heart desires

Is it for my kid or kids to want for nothing

But I'm tired

Dealing with all kinds of issues

Baby mother, court, unemployment, health issues

So much going through my mind

Thinking of going back to a life of crime

Drug dealing

I don't even have a dime

I made so many mistakes

Feel like a failure as a father

Wanting change

Wanting better

Wanting things to work together

I want my life back

I want my kids back

I want my family back

I want another chance

I'm trying to be a better man

Trying to do the best I can

<u>Trying To Live Right</u>

But I find that I sometimes fall out of line

Some things occupy my time

Some people take up my space

That prevents me from seeking your face

Trying to make some changes

Trying to do what is right

But there is a constant battle

A constant fight

Between what is right and what is wrong

Trying to let go and be strong

But I get tired because I been fighting for so long

Trying to live right

Trying to set my house in order

But I made a mistake

Now I have a daughter

Trying to do what is right

But I have some problems and issues in my life

Trying to do the right thing

Will God forgive me for the way I have been living

Trying to stop doing drugs

Trying to stop drinking

Is it too late to change is what I'm thinking

Trying to live right

I cheated on my wife

Trying to live right

I cause someone to die

Trying to live right

I end up in jail for life

God, you have to help me

I know you want me to come home

I have done everything wrong

I feel so alone

I am trying to live right

Trying to give up everything that doesn't matter

Trying to give you my all, my life

A New Thing

God will do a new thing

Which require change

Sometimes it brings hurt and pain

Causing you to bleed

Internal bleeding

While leading

Making hard decision

While trying to stick with the vision

God will do a new thing

Which requires moving ahead

Letting some things go

New mind

New goals

A new beginning

Mean some things will end

You might lose some friends

Your new direction

Will cause separation

You have a new destination

No longer will you bleed

Peace of mind

Your mind will be at ease

Don't look back

When doing a new thing

Everyone won't agree

Tough decisions will be made

God will do a new thing

Embrace your new day

Flashback

God reminding you of the past

Bringing to your memory how he saved you from the crash

The gun to your head

God stopped the bullet from firing

You should be dead

Don't forget the doctor's report

They discover a lump on your breast

We shall believe the lord report

The lump is gone

Flashback

God erases your past

All your sexual sins

All your wrongdoing

Flashback

Every time you think about getting out of line

Anytime you think about losing your mind

God reminds you of where he brought you from

What he brought you out of

He reminds you of his love

Every time you want to light up

Every time you want to give up

Flashback

Reminding you of the past

So you can get back on track

Flashback

Positive Quotes For Daily Living

- There will be no glory without a story. You will not go higher without going through the fire.
- Just because someone treats you right doesn't mean they are right for you.
- Many fall in LUST, not LOVE, which is why it is so easy for them to walk away.
- There's comes a point in time when your actions and not only words must show your support.
- Humble yourself; no matter how great you think you are; you have a flaw or weakness.
- The more you focus on what people think, the longer it will take you to get to where you're going.
- Your pain will reveal your gift.
- Pay attention to the consequences before you make your decision.
- Sometimes it is the people you want to hold on to that let go of your hand.
- People will REMEMBER what you USED to be, but they won't FORGET what you're GOING to be.
- Your elevation will create separation.
- Sex is expensive. Make sure you can afford it.

o Sometimes you have to be thankful for the NO you received because if you had said YES, you wouldn't be where you are today.

o Sometimes being happy for someone else hurts because it doesn't benefit you.

o It will make sense later. You don't understand why now. It will make sense later. What you are experiencing or have gone through will help others.

o Your PHYSICAL will get his attention, but your MENTAL is what will keep him interested.

o Excuses can hinder your wealth and happiness.

o Excuses can paralyze you and cause you not to walk into your purpose and destiny.

o Your gift is your presence. Not everyone is allowed to have this present.

o When you're a giver, "No" can be the hardest thing to say, but when you feel you are being taken advantage of, "No" becomes easy.

o When you have given so much to others, it's ok sometimes to be selfish.

o Loving people despite their mistakes is very important because one day, you will need the same love when you make your mistakes.

o Sometimes you must tell your feelings to shut up and have a seat. Feelings make you do things you thought you would never do. Make you say something you thought you would never say. Feelings make you regret some decisions. Feelings make you keep friends you should let go. Feelings make you hold on to a relationship because you love that person. Feelings take you through the twists and turns, hoping you don't crash and burn.

o Your freedom will come with a price, and sometimes it is painful, but when you are free from people and things that distract you, hinder you, or make you lose your mind, you can now help others be free.

o Sometimes to have peace of mind, you must let go of some people. I am doing what I must do because I choose freedom.

o Minding your business will keep stress out of your life. Know what to take on and when to walk away.

o Giving up on people is hard when the love of God is in you.

o You grow and mature when you can accept correction in love.

o You will experience your valley before you reach your mountain top.

o Most people still don't understand you and have known you for years.

o God will make you uncomfortable where you are when it's time for you to move on.

o God is waiting for us to realize who we are and move in.

o Your dream can't happen without a difficult journey.

o When you put God last, you will crash.

o Sometimes the person you're with is not the one you will marry.

o When you give life to something, you will experience pain first.

o If your tomorrow could talk, it would speak of the pain of your yesterday and be able to speak life into someone today and help them believe in their tomorrow.

o You will experience your CROSS before your RESURRECTION. On your journey to your cross, it will be painful and hurtful, and you will feel like you are alone and wonder if God has forsaken you, but do not worry; you will rise again.

o There is power in saying NO when you don't want to deal with the consequences of saying YES.

o Not everybody you know is your friend.

o Leaving some people alone will keep you mentally, emotionally, and spiritually healthy.

o Check your motive before doing something positive.

o Don't let your emotions lead you because sometimes, they can be the biggest liar.

o Being different sometimes means walking alone.

o Some people can say I LIKE YOU or I LOVE YOU and curse you with the same mouth behind your back.

o Your hurt and pain won't go to waste. It will help someone else later. You didn't go through what you went through for nothing.

o Sometimes rejection leads you to what is right.

o Rejection hurts but smile because they will regret rejecting you when they see what you will become.

o Be careful that you don't reject love when it's being offered because when you decide that you're ready to receive love, it may not be available.

o Sometimes love comes to visit, but it doesn't stay.

o One thing about the love of God that has been downloaded into your system is that whenever you try to not care about some people, God reminds you that it's all about him and not about you.

o There are times when you don't care; you erase your text message or inbox message and don't speak to a person; but God pushes you to reach out.

o Sometimes all someone need is your presence.

o Be careful of who you reject because you might regret it later.

o We are living in a time where cheating is easy and it hard to be faithful.

- The ones who can't STAND you will be SITTING at the table to celebrate your victory party. God is preparing your guest list.
- Sometimes the one you want close-up ends up being someone you must love from a distance.
- After you have done all, you can for people, sometimes you must walk away, so you don't lose your mind.
- Disappointment will work in your favor.
- Don't let loneliness lie to you and tell you that the wrong person is the right person.
- When you have been disappointed many times, you pull away, so you don't like, feel, or love.
- Sometimes you spend many years with who you want but will marry the one you need.
- When your heart is broken, your head doesn't work.
- Forgiveness isn't easy because memory makes it hard.
- Too many people get in the wrong relationship because they fall in love with the right things said by the wrong person. Words lie, so be deaf to what they say until their actions give you a reason to listen.
- For God's word to come to pass, some enemies will be revealed to you, and some people will turn on you.
- Paying attention + listening + actions = a woman smile.

o Sometimes people only remember you when you stop giving them your time and attention.

o Sometimes your mind is ready to decide what your heart is not ready to make.

o A relationship or friendship dies when you give it no time or life.

o Your new season is going to cause more people to dislike you.

o It's very easy to encourage others but very hard to encourage yourself.

o It takes one mistake to change someone's mind about you.

o Sometimes the people we trust the most are the people we shouldn't trust at all.

o No matter how much in love you are with someone, if they not helping you to GROW, they are causing you to SHRINK. If you're not a better person after being involved with someone, time to evaluate and make some changes.

o Sometimes you must fall back and see who is really for you and against you. Many will suck you dry. Many really don't want nothing to do with you. Many don't know what love and friendship are. Fall back, watch and observe. You will be surprised by what you see.

o Stay far away from people who talk bad about someone else but still hang around the person they talk bad about.

o Sometimes doing what is best for you will hurt others.

o When you love someone, you ought to leave room for them to make mistakes and love them despite.

o Your PAST will try to interfere with your PRESENT because it won't be a part of your FUTURE.

o Stay close to whoever inspires you and away from whoever drains you.

o Sometimes God teaches us how He loves us unconditionally by putting people in our lives that are not always easy to love. But we must love them anyhow. Unconditionally.

o Sometimes your taken to a LOW place so you can see who is with you while God is preparing you for the HIGH place.

o If you don't feel important, God reminded you this morning by waking you up.

o The gifts of a Godly woman never threaten a Godly man.

o The more people talk about you, lie about you, spread rumors about you, and speak negatively about you, give God more reason to take you higher and bless you more.

o A real man is one who can have fun with you, without being sexual.

o When you keep getting disappointed, hurt, and experiencing pain from one person time and time again, it's time to let them go.

o If someone is meant to be in your life, they'll come on their own.

- Anything or anybody that you love more than God, will be removed.
- As painful as your present is, your future is going to be worth every moment of it.
- Sometimes the best way to be there for somebody is to leave them alone.
- Never forget your friends when you're in a relationship.
- Be careful of confusing love with company. Some people just want your company and not your love.
- You are becoming wiser and better because you realize you don't need everybody in your life. Less people = more peace.
- Don't rush to get something that God is not ready for you to have.
- Sometimes no one can hear your silent scream.
- The people who hurt you the most are the ones you help.
- A person really loves and cares about you when they take the time to build a friendship with you.
- Don't keep a friendship alive that is meant to die. Know when that person's time is up in your life.
- The higher you go, the less friends you will have.
- Beware of someone who makes you feel guilty about what they're doing for you.
- Your singleness is your preparation period where God works on your emotional, mental, spiritual, and financial so that you

are prepared when he is ready to send his best for you. Rushing out of singleness will lead to brokenness.

o People will notice the change in you when you decide to lose the weight you carry. When you carry people and take on things God didn't give you, your mind, body, and spirit suffer. Now is the time to do what is best for you rather than what is best for others.

o Sometimes our hearts can be so big that we continue to be there for people who mean us no good.

o It's important that you take time for yourself to heal. Jumping from one relationship to the next without taking time to evaluate and check yourself and heal, will only hurt you and the next person you get involved with. It's like you taking off a band-aid before the bleeding stops.

o The hurt and pain of your cross will be nothing compared to the celebration of your resurrection.

o Just because someone is good to you in friendship doesn't mean they are for you in a relationship.

o You will tell who is fake and who is real because their heart will be revealed.

o Be careful not to hook up with anybody when you are broken.

o Get around people who know you and understand you and love you anyway. Get around people who see greatness in you and do their best to pull it out of you.

o You can't heal properly because you keep removing the band-aid.

o Few people will be with you in your valley, but everybody wants to be with you at your mountain top.

o Some people are paying for the consequences of a moment. Be careful of what kind of moment you create.

o Your mountain top is sweeter because you had a taste of the valley.

o Many people will have one view of you because they don't know you, but when they get to know you, they see a different side.

o Friendship is responsibility and accountability.

o Be careful who you throw away because you might need them in your personal famine.

o When you celebrate other people's success, your turn will come, but when you become envious and jealous, you hold up your own celebration party.

o Your hurt and pain are training for your future victory.

o Some people won't understand your story, so they won't be able to handle your glory.

o Lies will keep you talking, and the truth will keep you quiet. With truth, God is your defender, but with lies, you must defend yourself.

o You can't have one foot in yesterday, one foot in today, and expect to move into tomorrow.

o You are expensive. You are not cheap. You have been brought with a price. A price was paid so you can be here. That means you are valuable. You are worth it. Make sure the people in your life treat you that way, if they don't, they need to be removed.

o To make a difference, you got to be different. Don't label the person of your present as the same as the person of the past, they may be different. Everybody is not the same; renew your mind and thinking.

o Sometimes faithful people get hurt by ungrateful people.

o Your shift will be unexplainable. Many won't understand your change. Quit explaining.

o Sometimes things happen in our lives that only leave us with our peace of mind. But at that moment, you realize that your peace of mind means everything.

o It's not enough to speak love but to demonstrate it. Too many people have spoken empty words. Love demonstrated will never be forgotten.

o Some ingredients that show you have elevated are when you're talked about, misunderstood, mistreated, stabbed in the back, lied on, hated on, misused, or abused. Your elevation comes with a price.

- Your elevation will bring separation.
- The worst hurt is when the one or ones closest to you used to bless you but now curse you.
- Your Judas may have hurt you, but it can't break you.
- Your shift is going to reveal people's true colors.
- Your Judas will be revealed in your shift.
- Your shift is going to cause people to turn on you.
- Your shift will create enemies.
- God is shifting things in your life for the good; that is why there are changes happening and things falling apart.
- You're the answer to someone's problem. God is waiting for you to let him use you.
- Your procrastination is hurting others.
- The one God will choose is the one you bypass.
- Snakes bite when you least expect it.
- Two things God is waiting for you to do. He wants a Yes out of you and for you to let go and trust him.
- Your freedom doesn't begin until you are real with yourself.
- When you give people love, you give them Jesus
- The DARK times in your life will cause you to SEE things so clearly
- Some people speak the truth about you behind your back and lie right in front of your face.

o Beware of people who will publicly bless you but privately curse you.

o There are some bridges you don't burn because one day, you may have to cross over that bridge to get to your destination and may even have to pay a toll.

o To be happy, you must be free from what once made you happy.

o There is no happiness without peace. Don't lose your peace of mind trying to be happy.

o Sometimes to be happy, you must experience hurt for a season. But the hurt will be a learning experience that will help others because of where you're going and what you will become.

o As soon as you let go, God will release his blessing to you

o Everything is happening all at once in your life, God is up to something concerning you. Trust him all the way

o God is ending something that you thought was great to give you something that is greater.

o You're in an unusual place because it's time for you to move from your familiar, move to a new place, a new level. You're uncomfortable, and you're exactly where God wants you to be. Trust him and listen for instructions.

o It had to happen so you can grow

- What God is preparing you for is great; that is why you can't have just anybody

- God is preparing things for you, setting things up, and rearranging things in your favor.

- What happened to you wasn't meant to break you but make you.

- The signs that things are shifting in your life are when you're uncomfortable, your routine changes, people enter, people exit, and your life is turned upside down.

- Sharing so much of your personal life now with others can cause you to regret it later.

- God is speeding up the process in your life. Things are happening suddenly. The changes that are happening are for your good.

- God is going to give you double for what you lost.

- The second time around, they will notice your beauty, your gift, your value, and it will be too late.

- God is speeding up the process, you suffer for too long. Change will take place.

- Just when you feel like giving up, God will give you a reason not to.

- While many chases after titles and positions, those who aren't looking for them or don't even want them end up getting them.

o There is a time for church; a time for family; and a time for friends. Too many people's spiritual life is great, but their private life is out of order.

o No matter how nice and loving you are, you can't be friends with everybody

Matthew Bacchus is the founder of a Non-Profit Organization, Helping Others Meet Expectations (H.O.M.E). He is the author of a Poetry Book, "My Poetry, My Story, My Testimony, For His Glory and Co-author of Taking Care of Our Mental Health: From a Christian Perspective. Born and raised in Queens, NY by two wonderful parents Pastor Michael Bacchus and Patricia Bacchus. Mr. Bacchus attends Full Gospel Assembly in Brooklyn, NY, where he serves as Deacon. Matthew noted that Church has been his life for 39 years. He is grateful to have been brought up in a Christian environment which influenced my life and made him the man he is today.

Resources

- Alcoholics Anonymous
  1-800-923-8722
  New York City: 1-212-870-3400

- BETTERHELP.COM
  www.blackmentalhealth.com

- Better Urban Health LLC
  www.betterurbanhealth.com

  New York
  209 West 29th Street | Suite: 266 | NYC, NY | 10001 |
  646-600-4570
  Bronx
  1835 Westchester Avenue | Bronx, NY | 10472 |
  646-600-4570
  Kings
  400 Jay Street | Brooklyn, NY | 11201 |
  646-600-4570
  Queens
  46-28 Vernon Boulevard | Long Island City, NY | 11101 |
  646-600-4570
  Westchester
  1767 Central Park Ave South | Yonkers, NY | 10710 |
  646-600-4570
  Richmond
  2744 Hyland Boulevard | Staten Island, NY | 10306 |
  646-600-4570
  Niagara
  2430 Military Road | Niagara Falls, NY | 14304 |
  646-600-4570
  Erie
  2316 Delaware Avenue | Buffalo, NY | 14216 |
  646-600-4570
  Monroe

620 Park Avenue | Rochester, NY | 14607 |
646-600-4570
Onondaga
391 Nottingham Road | Syracuse, NY | 13210 |
646-600-4570
Oneida
186 N. Genesee Street | Utica, NY | 13502 |
646-600-4570
Rockland
228 East Route 59 | Nanuet, NY | 10954 |
646-600-4570
Dutchess
4 Marshall Road |Wappingers Falls, NY |12590 |
646-600-4570
Orange 367 Windsor Highway | New Windsor, NY |12553
646-600-4570
Nassau and Suffolk Co. 865 Route 58 | Riverhead, NY |
11901 | 646-600-4570

o B.O.N.D Bridging Our Natural Differences
Relationship & Personal Coach
http://www.bridgingournaturaldifferences.com/
bridgingournaturaldifferences@gmail.com
(347) 533-4174

o BULLYING
1800-420-1479
TEXT HOME to 741741

o BURNOUTBEGONE
Laura Smith, LCSW
Burnoutbegone@gmail.com
929-359-3014

o Domestic violence
1800-799-7233

Or
TEXT: SUPPORT to 741741

o Drug Addiction Center of Brooklyn
1-800-558-0175

o EATING DISORDERS
1800-931-2237
TEXT NEDA to 741741

o **GRIEF**
1800-445-4848
or
TEXT CARE to 839863

o Narcotics Anonymous (NA)
1-818-773-9999 or 212-929-6262

o WWW.NAMI.org
National Alliance on Mental Health
1800-950-6264
TEXT NAMI to 741741

o National Domestic Violence Hotline
PHONE: 1-800-799-7233 / 1-800-787-3224 (TTY)

o National Suicide Prevention Lifeline (24/7)
PHONE: 1-800-273-8255
CHAT: https://suicidepreventionlifeline.org/
INFO/CHAT: https://www.thehotline.org/

- o Mental Health First Aid
  1800-273-8256

- o S.A.Y. - The Stuttering Association for The Young
  www.say.org
  247 West 37th Street,
  5th Floor, New York, NY 10018.
  info@say.org.

- o SELF HARM
  1800-366-8288
  TEXT CONNECT to 741741

- o SUICIDE
  CALL 1800-273-8255
  TEXT: HELLO to 741741

- o SEXUAL ASSAULT
  1800-656-4673
  TEXT HOME to 741741

Made in the USA
Middletown, DE
07 September 2022

72669024R00080